Prefab and Modular

Prefabricated Houses and Modular Architecture

gestalten

The Timeless Wisdom of Prefabricated Architecture

Tracing the Evolution of Efficiency-Based Construction

Although we have embraced it as a hallmark of modern architecture, prefabrication is far from being a recent innovation. This practice—known for producing components in a controlled environment for later transportation and on-site assembly—is as old as the very essence of human ingenuity. Since ancient times, our ancestors easily grasped that this approach allowed them to achieve great results by reducing unnecessary efforts. Thus, the heart of prefabrication lies in the principles of efficiency, precision, and the proper use of available resources. Before delving into its fascinating history, which goes hand in hand with the narrative of human civilization, clarifying some fundamental concepts is essential.

To begin, it is important to understand the distinction between prefabrication and modular architecture. Although their concepts are often confused, modularity constitutes just one facet of the broader practice of off-site manufacturing. That is, in theory, all modular buildings are prefabricated, but not all prefabricated buildings are modular. In other words: a building can be factory-built as a unit or in large sections, but not necessarily through independent modules.

Are there different types of prefabrication? Yes, and they can be clearly classified, ranging from individual components (lower level of prefabrication) to complete buildings (higher level of prefabrication). For better clarity, let's review these different levels:

Components: At this level, basic units, such as beams, columns, doors, and windows, are manufactured off-site and then transported to the construction site for assembly.

Panels: Here, two-dimensional construction systems, such as floors, walls, and ceilings, are manufactured off-site and then transported to the construction site for assembly. Panels, and consequently the more advanced levels of prefabrication, can be pre-insulated and are typically constructed using materials like wood frames, steel frames, precast concrete, and even 3D printing.

Volumes: Entire spaces of a building (including bathrooms and kitchens) are manufactured off-site and then transported to the construction site for assembly. Each three-dimensional module is self-contained and functional and can be combined with other units to create a larger structure.

Hybrid Systems: Here, two-dimensional and three-dimensional components are combined to create a customized construction solution such as panels and volumes, for example.

Complete Building: Prefabrication is total. The entire structure is shipped from the factory and installed on pre-arranged foundations. While it reduces on-site work, its design is constrained by transportation logistics.

This book showcases the effective implementation of these prefabrication systems in 52 notable projects worldwide. Through a detailed exploration of their unique features and innovative approaches, it serves as an inspiring guide, demonstrating that efficiency is vital in the pursuit of good architecture.

Prehistory and Antiquity

An Ancient Practice Rooted in Common Sense

Against the odds, some 6,000 years ago, a group of skilled Neolithic builders had already instinctively employed prefabrication methodologies.

It all began when the first inhabitants of what we now know as the Somerset Levels in England were forced to find a way to navigate damp reed swamps. The answer came in the form of the "Sweet Track"—a subtle wooden causeway that stretched nearly 1.2 miles (2 kilometers). Meticulously designed, the walkway consisted of three basic components: a lower log rail, a series of crossed V-shaped posts for support, and an oak plank platform to walk on, anchored to the ground with wooden pegs. All elements were cut and pre-worked before being moved to their final location,

← Designed by Emil Tessin, the Frost House is a typical midcentury modern example of prefabricated housing.
↑ The Parthenon in Athens was constructed with the use of prefabricated elements.

minimizing material waste and facilitating assembly on muddy and unstable terrain. With over a decade of utility in the midst of a challenging climate, the success of this design is undeniable. However, the early feat of converting wood into standardized units underscores humanity's intrinsic drive for efficiency, which will become the main motivating force behind the evolution of prefabrication going forward.

As the centuries progressed, architectural works also grew in magnificence, forcing the search for building strategies suited to their complexity. Around 4,500 years back, craftsmen in Egypt undertook the monumental task of carving and assembling millions of stones, each weighing at least two tons, to create the impressive Egyptian pyramids. While the details of their construction are still a matter of debate, it is commonly agreed that these structures are a direct result of prefabrication. The enormous stones were prepared in quarries, which essentially functioned as factories producing pieces that were then transported to the worksite. Herodotus, a Greek historian who observed the pyramids around 450 BCE, is one of the oldest sources documenting these processes in his *Histories:* "Some of these [stones Amasis] got from the quarries over against Memphis, but the largest were brought from Elephantine, which is 20 days' voyage from Saïs." In the case of the white limestone exterior casing eroded by time, these far-off quarries were essential to achieve perfect symmetry, creating precise pieces of equal height and width. It is believed that these units were even labeled to indicate their specific angles, simplifying the installation process.

Centuries later, possibly drawing from their ancestors' experiences, other ancient civilizations harnessed the advantages of prefabrication in their monumental constructions. In both Greece and Rome, the first architects greatly refined their techniques, resulting in buildings of fine aesthetics and intricate detailing. The influential classical architecture flourished and, with it, new approaches to prefabrication emerged. A noteworthy example is the Parthenon in Athens, erected between 447 and 438 BCE, in which its fluted columns were meticulously assembled from individual pieces known as "column drums." These modules were pre-carved off-site, ensuring a precise fit that prevented any rotation or slippage, giving each column a spectacular monolithic effect.

Similar solutions—later replicated in coliseums, aqueducts, and even in medieval castles and churches—resonate deeply with human common sense: the simple yet transcendent wisdom of optimizing resources and streamlining processes. Guided only by their ingenuity and practical intelligence, the builders of ancient times paved the way for a practice that would transcend millennia.

The Renaissance

The Rebirth of Classical Architecture and the Consolidation of the Module

The Renaissance, a prolific era marked by a reevaluation of classical Greco-Roman elements, emphasized harmonic proportions, symmetry, and regularity, ushering in a transformative period for architecture and construction.

Unlike the Middle Ages, where master builders remained rather in darkness, in this era the figure of the architect was formalized, gaining greater social recognition. This is important in the evolution of prefabrication, as it marked the inception of architectural design and the planning of construction processes through the art of hand-drawing on paper. The discovery of perspective and the concept of the vanishing point generated new ways of understanding space, which could now be precisely measured and controlled.

One can notice that this is an era strongly marked by well-defined rules. Classical order was analyzed and documented, and architectural elements were classified to be used with balance and grace. As a result, the irregularity and roughness of early medieval buildings gave way to a systematic approach focused on modularity.

This element of modulation not only governed architectural design, but it was also crucial for the success of many constructions of the era, as they involved a multitude of intricate details and often took place in bustling urban centers. This was exemplified by the masterful Florence Cathedral's dome (1420–1436), envisioned by the Italian architect Filippo Brunelleschi. As the largest masonry dome ever raised, the project posed exceptional challenges. With a diameter of 149.3 feet (45.5 meters) and a height of 380.6 feet (116 meters), it was constructed without the use of scaffolding, compelling Brunelleschi to innovate revolutionary lifting systems. Historians recount that the dome's 28 marble ribs were carefully shipped from the distant Carrara quarry, where they were pre-sized and sculpted based on templates and models, possibly made of wood, clay, or wax. Treating the marble at the quarry helped reduce transportation costs, as only the finished blocks were transported to Florence—pure efficiency.

First Industrial Revolution

Prefab Pioneers: When Architects Met Machines

The next milestone in the evolution of prefabrication triggered transformations that reshaped the world. In the mid-18th century, society began to transition from a predominantly rural and agrarian economy to one centered around urbanization, industry, and mechanization. Great Britain, as the epicenter of this change, was the birthplace of a series of pivotal technological advances still relevant today, significantly expanding opportunities in construction. As architects encountered machines for the first time, they began to explore new aesthetic and functional possibilities in building design.

With the goal of celebrating the emerging modernity and showcasing the innovations of the time, important British figures organized the Great Exhibition of 1851 in London's Hyde Park. The main attraction of this event was precisely the building that housed it: Joseph Paxton's Crystal Palace. Representing a radical departure from conventional construction methods,

the imposing cast-iron and glass-plate structure was erected in just 39 weeks and became a milestone of prefabricated and modular architecture. As a reference, the brick and stone structure of the contemporary Buckingham Palace, with a similar floor area, took decades to build and more than a century to reach its current form.

Paxton's 990,000-square-foot (92,000-square-meter) design drew on his prior expertise in greenhouse construction, where he had already delved into module-based solutions. Not only was his design quick to install, but it also proved to be the most cost-effective among the proposed projects. Paxton took advantage of the booming iron and glass industries, using their ability to produce standardized elements that could be easily assembled on-site. The dimensions of the available glass panels, 9.8 × 47.2 inches (25 × 120 cm), directly influenced the shape and size of the entire building, establishing a foundational, self-supporting module of approximately 23.9 × 23.9 feet (7.3 × 7.3 meters) in surface area that was scaled from these measurements. This module could be indefinitely replicated to extend the building with no limits, or strategically omitted at certain points to create larger internal areas within the gallery. It even allowed for vertical stacking, generating double-height spaces on the second level.

At this point, the relationship between architects and manufacturers became indissoluble. Companies started to patent new products and technologies for commercialization, and, just as happened in the Crystal Palace, the available mass-produced elements began to strongly influence the more rational character of cities and built environments.

← The dome of the Florence Cathedral made history with its unparalleled size and revolutionary construction.
↑ A sketch of the Crystal Palace recalls the original presentation of the now-destroyed building.

Second Industrial Revolution

Architectural Masters Embrace Modular Design as It Goes Global

The Industrial Revolution continued its stride, and the transformative influence of reinforced concrete and steel came into play. Along with the refinement of machinery, these and many other unprecedented materials marked the onset of a new era in sophisticated mass production. Prefabrication, already recognized for its efficiency, began to transcend borders, aided by advancements in transportation and communication. Its versatility and time-saving benefits are perfectly aligned with the increasing demands of a growing global society, applied in critical structures like bridges, train stations, factories, and residential buildings.

In 1914, shortly after the outbreak of the First World War, the prominent Swiss-French architect Le Corbusier, assuming a short-lived conflict and foreseeing subsequent reconstruction efforts, designed the Dom-Ino House, a disruptive system that laid the foundations for modern housing. Its principles are genius yet simple: an open-plan structure composed of concrete slabs, stairs, and slender pillars. This framework eliminates load-bearing walls and roof support beams and is manufactured from standard elements that can be combined with each other, allowing countless home configurations. This approach separates the structure from the house plan and its functions, and envisions a prefabrication method that enables its modules and equipment to be shipped on demand.

As Le Corbusier himself reflected in his book *Œuvre complète*, this exploration not only influenced the way construction would later be conceptualized, but it also served as "a pretext for the first meditations on the imminent arrival of an international architecture." He wasn't wrong. In the following years, architectural luminaries developed valuable experimental projects of global impact based on modular design, driven by postwar economic limitations and housing shortages.

In the 1920s, German-American architect Walter Gropius, founder of the Bauhaus, used a children's game with geometric pieces as a basis for creating multiple construction kit systems. One of these was the so-called "Big Construction Kit," which was co-designed with Adolf Meyer in 1923. It comprised six basic modules of different sizes that could be combined to create houses in series in a variety of shapes. The concept emphasized the exceptional advantages of providing a "fixed price" and "definable construction times under warranty." At the end of the same decade, the concept of the Dymaxion House (1930) by American architect Buckminster Fuller was conceived. This 1,100-square-foot (100-square-meter) hexagonal home, intended to be affordable, transportable, and mass-produced, featured a lightweight structure supported by a central pole that could be shipped worldwide. Another noteworthy case is the 6 × 6 Demountable House by French architect Jean Prouvé, a concept developed in 1944 for post–Second World War homeless housing. The project, constructed from prefabricated pieces of wood and metal, was based on its patented axial portico and featured three

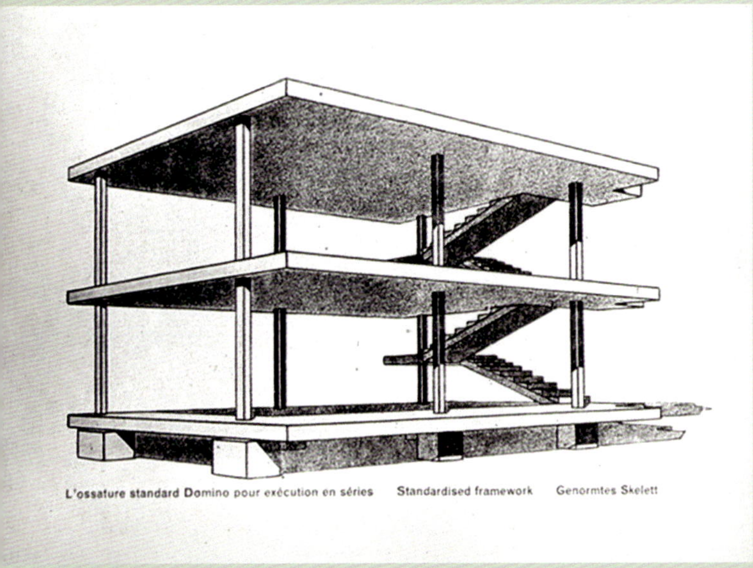

← Le Corbusier's Dom-Ino House pioneered open-plan, modular design for residential housing.
↑ The Steel House was designed for the Bauhaus in 1926 as an experiment in prefabricated construction.
→ The Eames House is one of the most well-known designs from the influential Case Study Houses Program.

rooms that were immediately habitable from the first day of construction.

It is crucial to mention the Case Study Houses Program (1945–1966), a series of residential architecture experiments developed by leading architects of the time. The intent was to create cost-effective and efficient model homes to accommodate millions of soldiers returning to the United States after the war. Many of these projects were built thanks to innovative prefabricated construction systems, promoting their subsequent development. One notable example is the Eames House designed by Charles and Ray Eames. Here, the architects were able to test "Cemesto," a pre-designed composite panel made from a sugarcane fiber insulating board core.

The postwar real estate boom not only inspired these and other renowned architects, such as Richard Neutra and Frank Lloyd Wright, to create iconic houses using prefabricated elements, but it also gave rise to a common image in magazines: ads offering prefab homes in the suburbs for young families. Some of the developed areas, like Levittown, New York, considered America's first suburb, reached construction rates of up to 30 houses per day in 1948.

Third Industrial Revolution

Digital Explorations Unleash the Potential of Prefabrication

When it seemed that almost everything had been said about prefabrication, the last two decades of the 20th century brought a transformative wave in the form of computer-aided design (CAD). These tools and other related software—known for their precision and increasingly sophisticated simulation capabilities—became indispensable allies for architects and engineers, who found in them the means to pre-design complex but easily replicable solutions.

In the midst of this digital explosion, experiments related to modular design were amplified. The Internet's immediacy led to a proliferation of bold prototypes coming from the academic world and from ideas exchanged at international events such as biennials and forums. This shift was evident in many of the winners of international architecture competitions, where juries began to prioritize projects that could be built quickly, economically, and efficiently. The debates

around these revolutionary concepts not only challenged conventional norms, but they also served as a testament to the limitless potential of prefabrication.

Modular kits for housing and urban equipment, previously presented as postwar solutions, were consolidated as marketable products. This multiplied the number of companies focused on offering solutions tailored to people's recurring needs and desires beyond their specific context. Some preferences translated into best-selling typologies, which also began to influence the way cities would be shaped.

The viral spread of trends worldwide found a good match in the replicability of certain popular prefab living models. The fever for tiny houses, maximizing interiors that barely exceed 325 square feet (30 square meters), evolved into a social movement with broad media support, founded on the ideology of living with less. Micro-homes can offer a pleasant off-grid, community-centered lifestyle for many, although their proliferation in dense urban areas raises concerns about potential overcrowding and the need to respect certain minimum quality of life standards. Another associated trend is the reuse of shipping cargo containers to convert them into living spaces. This approach has been valued for taking advantage of pre-existing structures that might otherwise be wasted, however its popularity has declined due to size restrictions, retrofit complexities, and difficulties in complying with local regulations.

All these new ideas have emerged and evolved thanks to the current ease of sharing knowledge. In this vast sea of information, some solutions have thrived while others have faded. However, in our fast-paced globalized world, prefabrication continues to offer relevant solutions that, when well thought out, can make a difference.

Fourth Industrial Revolution

Tech-Enhanced Prefabrication for Human-Centric Architecture

In past decades, modules were first designed in CAD and then built in the real world. Now, the integration of digital and physical processes has merged into a unified intelligent operation. This evolution is evident in the refinement of prefabrication methods through technologies such as 3D printing, virtual and augmented reality, artificial intelligence, and data-driven design. Today, we not only have the capacity to build numerous houses daily but also to do so in a smart, sustainable way in line with changing societal and environmental needs.

In short, 3D printing allows for the direct creation of three-dimensional objects from digital models, while artificial intelligence harnesses data to analyze designs, optimize material usage, and perform real-time quality checks. Virtual and augmented reality facilitate comprehensive process simulation, reducing errors in advanced stages. We have now reached a point where the promise of efficiency, eagerly sought by those who came before, seems to be virtually infallible.

With the unprecedented support of all these technologies, how could prefabrication principles amplify their positive influence on future human endeavors? This book sheds light on these opportunities by highlighting the powerful work of a range of modern architects. In the Warm Nest health center in Belgium (see p. 100), the architects of Ark-Shelter + Archekta demonstrate that, despite its rationality, the use of a single, standardized module for ease of construction still allows the creation of a space that is experienced in a fluid, organic way. In this case, the indoor environment was designed to warmly promote the health and well-being of patients and their loved ones at different physical and emotional stages. Another project that shows that prefabricated elements are not synonymous with rigidity—rather stimulating a high quality of life and adaptability—is the Sneglehusene housing in Denmark by the Bjarke Ingels Group (see p. 82). The building is simply the well-planned stacking of two types of residential modules, generating spacious rooms and including a terrace for each unit. The modules are cleverly arranged around a central public space that encourages community life. Prefabrication is not opposed, then, to the customization that every architectural project demands; instead, prefab structures can strategically complement each other to offer optimized and tailored solutions, successfully meeting the needs of specific users.

An exceptional case in this sense is that of the renowned Japanese architect Shigeru Ban. Driven by a deep social conviction, he has made the most of prefabrication and modular design to provide shelter and community facilities to those who urgently need them. Extremely easy to assemble and dismantle, his projects have delivered quality equipment to refugees and victims of natural disasters across all continents. Although he has experimented with materials such as bamboo, compressed earth blocks, and reused containers, his most successful strategy has been the use of lightweight structures made from paper tubes. These beautiful round pieces arrive ready to be assembled on-site; after fulfilling their function they can be repurposed into new projects.

The world is facing increasingly recurring crises, and some issues will require special attention from architects, such as the housing shortage, access to critical public infrastructure, or the adaptation of buildings to drastically changing lifestyles and urban contexts. Maybe it is not about reinventing the wheel, but rather about placing the human being and nature at the center, thus making the right decisions that allow us to achieve more with less—and with great efficiency.

Just like our ancestors, guided by intuition.

—José Tomás Franco

↞ Bjarke Ingels Group's Sneglehusene is a fully prefabricated neighborhood.
↖ Jean Prouvé's Demountable House provided shelter for the homeless after the Second World War.
← Ark-Shelter+Archekta's Warm Nest is a prefabricated care center.
↑ A Shigeru Ban shelter is displayed at a humanitarian architecture exhibit in 2014.

019 Cabin

ŠA Atelier
Apple Island,
Lithuania

Currently perched on a hill in Lithuania, the prefabricated 019 Cabin can be disassembled and transported anywhere. Compact and with a modernist design of glass and steel, the cabin was originally fabricated in a workshop and only later brought to the island. Its core framework includes two double bedrooms, a living room, a kitchen, and a bathroom economically distributed across only 248 square feet (23 square meters) of space. To achieve a flexible yet functional design, ŠA Atelier divided the cabin into modular components, separating the columns, floors, walls, and roofs. The structure is consequently both portable and rearrangeable, allowing for modest adjustments across locations. 019 Cabin is configured to perfectly suit its unique site: the roofs, which look like they are floating, protect it from the overhead sun; they also collect rainwater—useful in Lithuania's rainy climate. A furnished terrace faces the nearby lake, and the mirrored-glass back wall reflects the beautiful surrounding landscape.

Floating roofs and a fully mirrored glass wall set this otherwise simple, modern design apart.

←↙ 019 Cabin's minimalist, wooden interior opens to a covered terrace with seating. From there, users can lounge and enjoy the beautiful surrounding forest.
→ At night the structure softly glows, illuminating nearby trees.
↓↘ Unique geometric fixtures and furnishings make the cabin's limited space feel luxurious.

Living Unit

Ofis Architects
Ljubljana, Slovenia

Unlike many other prefabricated projects, Ofis Architect's Living Unit does not sacrifice unique aesthetics for efficient, portable construction. Composed of horizontally and vertically combinable modules, the project's basic unit is an asymmetrical polygonal section with large protruding windows. Each module is constructed with wood frames reinforced by plywood boards on each side; the exterior boards are sleekly painted black, enhancing its futuristic appearance. Inside, furnishings are fashionably compact, though precise treatments are variable. The standard design contains a bed, wardrobe, table, and chairs, accommodating two inhabitants, though combined modules can hold up to six. Living Unit is adaptable to a variety of different environmental conditions. Its small size ensures easy transportability and it can be fixed to the ground either by steel anchors or removable concrete cubes. The eccentric design lends itself to cabins, hideaways, treehouses, and other short-term shelters.

← Seen from afar, Living Unit stands out with its irregular geometry and textured wood facade.

↑ Square windows extrude from each end of the structure's component modules, allowing natural light in.

Still Life

← Interior furnishings cleverly combine functions to optimize limited space. Here, a kitchen counter doubles as stairs and storage. →↘ Living Unit's sleek, geometric aesthetic extends from its facade to its interior fixtures, including its window seating and bespoke appliances.

Gaia

Pin-Up Houses
Czech Republic

While the field of architecture has dramatically improved in terms of sustainability, many eco-friendly designs still cause environmental damage, however minimal. Gaia, a tiny, recycled shipping-container house, provides a model for truly sustainable living: fully self-sufficient, it comes with its own solar panels, wind turbine, and rainwater retention system. Making economical use of very limited space, the design incorporates plenty of storage, a convertible sofa bed, tables and chairs, a full bathroom, a kitchen, and even a retractable outdoor terrace. Of course, the container is also fully insulated. To help facilitate its functions, Gaia makes prudent use of available technologies. The home's batteries, energy use, charging, and more can be monitored through a mobile app. However, construction is left to the purchaser; designed for the truly dedicated, Gaia is sold as a set of plans and books—a DIY project for those invested in sustainable, natural, off-the-grid living.

This constructed example of the Gaia prototype demonstrates its DIY charm with unpainted, dynamic walls.

↖← With such minimal space, functionality is essential. Gaia's eccentric shelving units, wall pegs, and multifunctional furniture ensure maximum usability.
→ Nooks for a bathroom and kitchen area mark different sections of the home. Large sliding glass doors allow for plenty of natural light.

Pin Up
Houses

Dot House

Boano Prišmontas
London, U.K.

This prefabricated micro-home cozily sits in the garden of a North London row house. Compact and freestanding, this single-room unit, complete with a bathroom, was designed for multi-functionality: it can be used for entertaining or housing guests, or can serve as a tranquil place to study or work. One wall incorporates bespoke home office furniture, including cabinets, a desk, and a hidden computer station. A large motorized projector screen in front of this wall can transform the room into an intimate home theater. The interior's exposed plywood finishings complement the corrugated panels of black fiber cement that comprise the building's facade; together, they generate a modern, economical style. Dot House was entirely premanufactured in Prišmontas's London workshop and assembled in one day on-site. Its glass 10-foot-wide (3-meter-wide) patio doors were oriented toward the main house. A skylight brings gentle natural light into the narrow, terrazzo-tiled bathroom. Altogether, the micro-home is highly functional, tasteful, and unique.

↖ Dot House provides a comfortable, secluded nook for work and study. When not in use, the desk can fold away.

↑ The micro-home also includes large sliding glass doors, a sofa, and pegboard-based shelving.

← Dot House perfectly fits into this quaint North London garden, giving it a distinctive, chic look.
↑ The flexible pegboard shelving that dots this unit's walls inspired its charming, unusual name.
→ Cabinets surround the desk for extra storage, and a motorized projector screen sits overhead.

Bee House

Boano Prišmontas
U.K.

Although the Bee House was digitally prefabricated, its bee-inspired design feels artisanal. Designed as a versatile garden studio, the structure's raw wood aesthetic, thick black-frame windows, and modular textures present a stripped-back, contemporary take on a beehive's honeycomb. Each component serves a function: the gridded ceiling coffers hold acoustic wood-wool panels; the curving columns brace movable shelves between them; the pegboard-like wall texture supports additional flexible shelving; and the tall, sloping ceiling provides ample room for physical activities. An extruded window seat with a cork surface provides a warm and light-filled reading nook. The Bee House is a friendly reminder that digital fabrication and modular design can enhance our relationship with nature rather than hindering it.

↖ Bee House's warm brown walls and regular pegboard patterns loosely mimic a beehive's honeycomb.

↑ From the outside, the studio's wood facade and simple shape beautifully harmonize with the garden.

My Room in the Garden

Boano Prišmontas
U.K.

My Room in the Garden is a small prefabricated home office designed for backyard gardens, courtyards, usable rooftops, and pocket parks. Responding in part to the Covid-19 pandemic and the rise of the "work from home" model, it transports the workspace outside the main home and frees potentially limited domestic space. The pod is cozy and reasonably compact, sitting at 8.2 feet (2.5 meters) tall with just under 48 square feet (4.5 square meters) of floor space. It is constructed with corrugated clear polycarbonate cladding alongside wall materials of each buyer's choosing; the resulting interior is airy and light, open enough to let the sun in yet closed enough to feel like an escape. The walls are lined with digitally fabricated birch plywood modules that can be tailored to each customer's needs, customizable with desks, shelves, stands, and stools. Common to each component is the minimization of material waste, making My Room in the Garden both low-cost and sustainable.

↖ Digital fabrication allows for precise, distinctive wall and shelving patterns inside this premade pod.

↑ My Room in the Garden's small size makes it highly versatile and usable, even within a limited space.

Bubble House

Jean-Benjamin Maneval / Chzon
Vexin, France

Jean-Benjamin Maneval's prefabricated Bubble House, produced in the 1960s, is a gem from the much-beloved retro-futurist era. Constructed out of six prefabricated polyester shells, some fitted with Plexiglas window inserts, the organic design reminds us that prefabrication isn't always just rectangles and squares. A collector purchased the Bubble House at auction in 2014, after which the new owner commissioned Chzon to refurnish the home. The resulting interior captures the ethos of Maneval's original design: the furniture—all designed and manufactured specifically for this project—is as bubbly and eccentric as the home's larger form. In fact, their fun colors and odd shapes breathe new life into the bubble-like frame. These varied furnishings define the shells' different functions, demarcating a shower, bath/dressing room, bedroom, bar, living room, and an entryway. These areas all come together around a dining table at the Bubble House's center.

Bubble House's soft, bulging forms and irregular windows lend to its eccentric, retro-futurist aesthetic.

← Guests enter the house by ascending a set of stairs and crossing through a spaceship-like entry portal. Plexiglas windows offer a glimpse inside.
→↘ Pastel colors, varied textures, and vintage furnishings breathe new life into this restored relic of the retro-futurist era.

Te Pae

Crosson Architects
North Piha, New Zealand

Erected on the coast of New Zealand, Te Pae—meaning "to perch" in the indigenous Māori language—is a striking yet functional lifeguard tower surveilling the adjacent North Piha beach. Designed with panoramic windows, Te Pae provides sweeping views for up to four lifeguards at once. In turn, the tower is itself highly visible, signaling its location to approaching visitors and swimmers. Oddly, North Piha's sand is black, a peculiarity mimicked by Te Pae with its black oxidized concrete walls. The tower's shape also references traditional maritime structures dotting other parts of the New Zealand coast. Sections of the building were prefabricated and assembled on-site, leaving minimal impact on the immediate environment. The tower commits to sustainability with its ventilating windows, quality insulation, sun protection, thermal mass, and use of natural light. Despite its futuristic look, Te Pae embraces and protects the vast surrounding nature.

Te Pae juts out from the New Zealand coastline like the periscope of a submarine, surveying the waters.

←↓ Inside, the tower is dark and minimalist, punctuated only by soft lights and windows. The atmosphere is serene, and the design is highly functional.
→ Panoramic windows cut across Te Pae's cylindrical crown, offering uninterrupted views of the beach. These windows open for ventilation when needed.

Studio House

William Samuels Architects
Nelson, New Zealand

Architect William Samuels was directly confronted with New Zealand's over-inflated housing market when he first began looking for a home. His values of living small, sustainability, and, of course, affordability coalesced within the house he finally designed: Studio House. It is small enough to be transported yet livable as a permanent residence for Samuels and his partner. Because of its modularity, it can be expanded as the couple's needs grow while limiting resource and energy expenditure in the present. This commitment to sustainability extends to the home's materials (primarily natural) and even to its finishings (no paint is used). Despite the sparing method of design and construction, the house is chic and comfortable. Its large windows and deck belie the limited space by opening the home to the surrounding expanse. Studio House demonstrates that sustainable, affordable, and small living is not only possible—but that it can be wonderful, too.

The house's modular design allows it to be transported and expanded as its owners' needs evolve.

← Studio House makes use of multiple levels and flexible partitions to maximize utility. The lofted bed sits in a nook ensconced by the unique arched roof. →↓ Modern furniture and fixtures contribute to the distinctive aesthetic. The warm wood paneling and cool furnishings appear both natural and elegant.

“Tin Can” Castle

Kosmos Architects
Georgia

In response to an inflow of Ukrainian refugees into Georgia, the architecture firm Kosmos designed this rapid-construction, low-material housing module for those rendered homeless by war. The “Tin Can” Castle makes innovative use of very limited materials: boulders, tires, and found building materials comprise much of each structure. Tires act as foundations; boulders ensure stability, even in high wind; and scrap wood combines into frames. Other materials were all locally purchased. Because of the minimal construction requirements, anyone can help erect these shelters. In fact, the goal for these units is not just to create temporary homes, but to foster community. Despite the use of found materials, the “Tin Can” Castle looks chic and even futuristic. Large windows provide ample natural light for inhabitants. Crucially, each module is designed to be combinable, ensuring that larger buildings can be constructed as the need for space grows.

Tires, boulders, and scrap metal are among the materials that make these makeshift shelters function.

Sprout

Woonpioniers
Netherlands

The standard designs of each Sprout house are meant to function as an initial, flexible concept. From this base, individuals, families, and communities can expand on their own unique visions for these integrated homes and gardens. At its most fundamental level, Sprout is comprised of two sections. This first is a bare, prefabricated timber frame insulated with flax into which clients (with the help of the architects) can insert customizable rooms and levels. The second is a greenhouse extension that can function as a veranda or self-sufficient garden. The size and other key features of the home can change depending on each user's needs. The singular Sprout houses cater to individuals and families passionate about gardening, but they can also be combined to form a Sprout "village," making green-energy and self-sufficient living much more feasible. A few Sprout homes have already been purchased and constructed, revealing the degree to which they can be modified to meet different needs.

Sprout's two discrete zones, the home and the garden/veranda, produce a distinctively sectioned facade.

← The greenhouse extension opens from the main home, continuing the sloped roof with open beams and glass. This version uses a pleasant wood frame.

↓→ In this example, the owners opted to use the greenhouse extension as a furnished pseudo-veranda with a second level, an enclosed room, and patio doors.

Abodu One

Abodu
San Carlos, CA, USA

Abodu's fully outfitted backyard dwellings modernize and miniaturize the traditional gable-roofed house form. With slanted roofs and raked gables, polygonal windows, and cathedral ceilings, these homes look and feel both familiar and new, taking a well-loved design and injecting it with a dash of extra presence. Though the Abodu dwellings are compact—each comes fully equipped with a kitchen, bedroom, bathroom, and living room, but can range from just 340 to 800 square feet (35 to 74 square meters)—they tend to feel comfortable, even spacious. Part of the magic comes from the high ceilings and strategic window placement, which maximize the inflow of natural light. Buyers also have the option of adding folding panoramic doors, which quite literally expand the living room into the outdoors. In fact, buyers are given a whole suite of customization options, from the siding color and material to the types of flooring installed. Though prefabricated, Abodu dwellings are meant to feel like home.

These homes combine Scandinavian and Californian aesthetics with minimalist forms and natural wood facades.

←↙ Each house features sleek, high-contrast interior design punctuated with modernist fixtures and appliances. Irregular windows diffuse natural light.

↓ This iteration of the design includes external decking, accessible via folding glass doors. Selected furniture complements the home's minimalist aesthetic.

Kirkland Avenue Homes

Schemata Workshop
Renton, WA, USA

Erected in 2015, the Kirkland Avenue Homes were at the time the largest publicly funded affordable housing project in the state of Washington using modular construction. Designed for veterans and low-income families, the complex includes 14 two-bedroom townhomes and four three-bedroom apartments. Each building was constructed cost-consciously and with sustainability in mind. Rain gardens aid with storm water retention; the homes run on hydroelectric power; and over 75 percent of all construction waste was recycled. Large windows provide ample natural light in a climate prone to gray, rainy weather. From the outside, the complex's cheery colors and sleek design inject vibrancy into the neighborhood, too. The Kirkland Avenue Homes provide an impressive model for affordable public housing that maintains high standards for comfort, aesthetics, and sustainability—a crucial reminder that these three features should be necessary for all homes, not just luxury ones.

← The townhomes on Kirkland Avenue include multiple levels and large windows to optimize light.

↑ The complex's colorful facades and polygonal volumes lend a lively profile to the neighborhood.

1518 N
1518 M

Revival

Zikzak Architects
Ukraine

Zikzak Architects, recognizing the enormous infrastructural destruction in Ukraine following the 2022 Russian invasion, quickly moved to theorize efficient and affordable ways of reconstructing their war-torn country. Their solution, Revival, presents prefabricated and modular design as a means by which Ukraine can quickly rebuild lost schools, homes, and other essential structures. Each modular unit, which consists of wall, ceiling, and floor slabs in a steel frame, can be stacked and arranged to create a variety of building types. These quick constructions can function as temporary or permanent structures, and they can also be moved, adapted, and rearranged as needed. This versatility and reusability bakes sustainability into the very core of Ukraine's reconstruction. With the effect of the war's enormous rupture in Ukrainians' lives, Zikzak offers a much-needed solution to the vitally urgent project of fast recovery.

↖ In this rendering of one possible configuration, modules are stacked and connected across several axes.

↑ Modules can be used for a variety of functions, including community and family centers, as depicted here.

LET'S START
EXPERIMENT?

Pop Kudamm

Graft
Berlin, Germany

Thirty-five shipping container modules, all finished with a shiny silver coating, compose this temporary pop-up space in Berlin. Designed for exhibitions, performances, pop-up shops, lectures, and other cultural events for the City West community, Pop Kudamm is loosely organized into five sections, each with varying functions and capacities. The Creative Village, which surrounds the entrance, consists of 20- and 40-foot (6- to 12-meter) containers intended for retail use. The Main Hall, rooted at the center of Pop Kudamm, can hold up to 200 people for large-scale events. Two other spaces on the first floor can host small workshops, panels, and film screenings, while the "backyard" may accommodate performances, concerts, and larger open-air film showings. Pop Kudamm's modularity may ease deconstruction when the complex's tenure eventually ends, but its unique design also contributes to the space's chic, modern, and dynamic sensibility at present.

← Neon lighting mixes with sleek silver shipping containers at the eye-catching entrance.

↑ The complex's funky industrial aesthetic both complements and stands out from the surrounding area.

↓ Inside the main hall, stacked shipping containers compose multiple levels and rooms for programming.

→ The "backyard" includes amphitheater seating and space for performances, concerts, and film screenings.

Manifesto Market Anděl

Chybik+Kristof
Prague, Czech Republic

Designed to echo the courtyard style of Prague's unique urban design, Manifesto Market Anděl has an explicitly local focus. This playful marketplace and gathering space reactivates a neglected area in Anděl, Prague, with bars, restaurants, event spaces, and even a swimming pool. Beyond its cheerful blue scaffolding—which, near the center of the complex, functions as a terrace—the market also sits on an elevated wooden platform, gesturing to the unity of the space despite its openness. Each modular booth is wrapped in the same corrugated aluminum, and furniture styles remain relatively consistent across the complex. In fact, the furniture, lighting, and modular booth units are all on their second life, having first been used for the Manifesto Market in Smíchov (another neighborhood in Prague). Evidently dedicated to sustainability, Manifesto Market Anděl is also fueled by clean energy from renewable sources and, due to its modularity, can be easily reused again.

The small swimming pool at the center of Manifesto Market Anděl is a popular gathering space.

CLARINS
ArgenTINAS

↓ The modular retail booths and their furnishings were recycled from a previous iteration of the market.

→ The web of turquoise-blue scaffolding lends a unified, idiosyncratic look to the complex.

Modular Research Center

Chybik+Kristof
Vizovice,
Czech Republic

Skirting the edge of the KOMA Modular factory complex, the Modular Research Center both functions as an innovation hub for modular design strategies and embodies those strategies with its own unique approach to modular construction. The architects forwent traditional rectangular modules, instead fabricating them in unorthodox shapes for greater adaptability. While the interior remains relatively open, it avoids the disadvantages of open-plan offices through flexible, modular furniture that can be rearranged to form individual workstations, conference tables, and other formats as needed. Ceiling-mounted curtains augment this built-in versatility. Additionally, the Modular Research Center was not only built for research, but also to facilitate a connection between the complex and its surrounding community. As such, the center includes a semi-public gathering space outside, and the building itself is highly transparent with its floor-to-ceiling windows and open plan.

The Modular Research Center is itself an experiment in non-rectilinear modular design.

←↙ The center features a green roof, sliding glass doors, and ceiling-mounted curtains alongside its office furniture, arranged in a semi-open floor plan.

↓ Many of the desks and chairs have wheels, permitting flexible configurations. The nooks formed by the irregular modules help partition the otherwise open space.

Mendel's Greenhouse

Chybik+Kristof
Brno, Czech Republic

Gregor Mendel, a 19th-century friar and scientist who was posthumously dubbed the founder of modern genetics, conducted his groundbreaking experiments in a greenhouse at St. Augustin Abbey. This greenhouse was swept away by a storm in the 1870s, though its foundations endured. In 2022, to commemorate the 200th anniversary of Mendel's birth, Chybik + Kristof constructed Mendel's Greenhouse over the historic structure's foundation. The versatile new building—primarily dedicated to a permanent exhibition on Mendel's legacy—also hosts conferences, lectures, and other cultural events. Its remarkable redesign borrows from the original greenhouse's unique shape, while its new modular steel roof imitates the linear and nodal schemes of Mendel's famous laws of inheritance. As such, the very design of Mendel's Greenhouse—not only its contents—pays homage to the pathbreaking Czech scientist.

This design both echoes Mendel's original experimental greenhouse and updates it for the present day.

Sneglehusene

Bjarke Ingels Group
Aarhus, Denmark

With the Sneglehusene, which translates to "snail houses," the Bjarke Ingels Group proves that modular, prefabricated construction can provide beautiful and functional housing at an urban scale. This six-building, curving complex is located in the Aarhus neighborhood of Nye and challenges the format of the traditional city block. Constructed instead in a spiral shape resembling a snail's shell, the complex centers around a public pond and shared community gardens. The modular design of the apartments allowed for efficient construction and constituted the refined checkered facade of the Sneglehusene. Much like the shape of the complex, water is collected and consumed in a circular fashion. The pond collects rainwater runoff, provides it to a local water plant, and sends the purified water back to the residents. This new neighborhood is an ambitious yet functional experiment in sustainable, modular urban planning.

Sneglehusene's modular units surround a pond and gardens, integrating public space into the neighborhood.

↓ Apartments in the complex feature sleek, minimalist interior design, exuding quiet luxury. Primary materials include wood and concrete, offset with white paint.
→ Large floor-to-ceiling windows open units to plentiful natural light and expansive views of the pond, gardens, and neighborhood complex.

← Sneglehusene's distinctive spiral shape recalls the pattern of a snail's shell.
↓ Apartments open to terraces and shared gardens; many include green roofs.
→↘ The neighborhood's expansive, multilevel apartment units come with integrated appliances, abundant storage, and contemporary light fixtures.

1000 m² Prefabricated Housing

Summary
Vale de Cambra, Portugal

This multi-use housing complex, located on a public roadside, used prefabricated and modular building systems to facilitate quick, cost-effective construction. The structure includes two levels: the ground floor, which connects directly to the street, was designed for a multiservice non-residential program; above it, individual housing units are accessible from the opposite direction, taking advantage of the sloping terrain. The ground floor interior is flexibly arranged using removable panels to anticipate changing needs. The residential units, though part of a collective housing program, are separate and freestanding, providing further privacy. To ensure rapid and efficient construction, each unit—including insulation, water, and electricity—was fully constructed in a factory and simply transported on-site. Called the "Gomos System" by Summary, the project's construction system and multi-unit plan convincingly responds to evolving social and architectural needs.

The six residential units crowning the complex are distinguished by their unusual polygonal shapes.

← The housing units rest atop a large nonresidential space.
↙ Yellow partitions demarcate rooms inside each apartment, complementing the raw concrete ceilings and walls.

↓ The operable floor-to-ceiling windows that cap each apartment of 1000 m² Prefabricated Housing allow for abundant natural light and ventilation.

Land on Water

Mast
Lake Constance, Austria

The climate crisis is not a distant apocalypse for future generations to worry about—it is happening now. Responding to rising sea levels and urban flooding around the world, Land on Water envisions a modular floating foundation system that can support several different building types—on water. These can range from residential communities to leisure centers such as parks, cafes, and campsites. Many current floating building solutions suffer from inflexible and unsustainable construction materials: polystyrene-filled concrete foundations and steel pontoons, for example, are often treated with toxic protective paints. By contrast, Mast plans to make its easily transportable modules from recycled plastic and fill them with locally sourced materials; underneath, the floats are additionally designed as ideal habitats for aquatic life, promoting biodiversity. Inspired by an ancient construction technology called gabion construction, Land on Water will sustainably adapt traditional design for urgent contemporary needs.

This rendering imagines how a residential community supported by the floating foundation system would look.

↞ Ideally, the foundations could hold not just man-made constructions, but parks and other forms of nature, too.
← This drawing depicts the system's underside: trusses demarcate segments in which buoyant materials are placed.
↓ The modules, made of recycled plastic, are easy to transport and assemble.

AKA Patagonia

Larrou Arq
Puerto Natales, Chile

Seven unpretentious wooden modules constitute this unique hotel in the Patagonia area of Chile, a region renowned for its beautiful natural landscapes. Emerging from the ground like mountains, volcanos, or glaciers, these unique structures pay tribute to the region's distinctive terrain while providing unfettered access to that very same land. Six of the modules serve as private double rooms for guests, while the seventh offers space for communal gatherings, cooking, and general relaxation. Each room includes large windows that spotlight panoramic views of the otherwise uninterrupted scenery. The hotel's construction left a minimal environmental impact: modules were prefabricated and then assembled over piles to limit ecological damage, and the primary material used was locally sourced lenga wood. Over time, the wood will age—without structural deterioration—alongside its environment to truly integrate the hotel with its breathtaking surroundings.

← From afar, the modules of AKA Patagonia resemble the surrounding mountains and glaciers.

↑ Each module functions either as a private double room or communal space, connected by a wooden walkway.

← The hotel's interiors adopt a natural, minimalist aesthetic.
↙↓ Large windows pair with the pale lenga wood to create a soft, pleasant atmosphere.
→ The communal gathering area, which includes dining and seating areas and a functional kitchen, offers space for guests to cook, talk, and relax.

Warm Nest

Ark-Shelter+Archekta
Knokke-Heist, Belgium

Designed in consultation with medical professionals, Warm Nest eschews the typically sterile, uninspiring design of hospital architecture to create a space that is truly healing in its atmosphere. With warm walls, numerous skylights, large windows, and lush courtyards, this cancer care center is meant to feel homey and welcoming, soothing ill patients and their families during what might be the most difficult time of their lives. Each room—whether an office, therapy room, or dining space—varies in intimacy, privacy, and flexibility according to the patients' anticipated needs. Built primarily with wood and constructed out of uniform, prefabricated modules, Warm Nest is thus sustainable in a material sense but also in a human sense, leaving no environmental footprint and actively restoring its users' health. Though beautiful, the center's foremost aim is to help patients, mobilizing the affective qualities of architecture to ensure their utmost comfort—and hope.

This care center is composed of a 12-module grid, with two modules that vertically stack.

← Large windows in every room open onto interior courtyards and the lush surrounding landscape.

↓ Skylights and other carefully placed sources of ambient natural light cast the interior in a soothing glow.

Uni Kanava Resort

Studio Puisto
Oravi, Finland

Nine of Studio Puisto's prefabricated Uni Villas were built for the Kanava Resort on the shores of the Oravi canal in Finland, forming a luxury holiday destination in a beautiful rustic setting. Each villa is constructed with natural materials, including cross-laminated wood that casts the interior in a warm glow that harmonizes with the forest scenery. The dark wooden exteriors resemble the bark of a pine tree while enormous floor-to-ceiling windows facilitate magnificent views of the water. Each villa's modular construction simultaneously optimized resource efficiency for the architects and resort. At the same time, the villas are certifiably luxurious. Each unit includes a small sauna while the living spaces can accommodate groups of up to six people. The villas' U-shaped assembly leaves space for a private courtyard secluded from other units. Whereas Kanava Resort had originally intended to build a hotel on the site, the Uni Villas provide an efficient yet lavish alternative.

Each unit contains living quarters for up to six alongside a private sauna and courtyard.

Arctic TreeHouse Hotel

Studio Puisto
Rovaniemi, Finland

This extension of the Arctic TreeHouse Hotel in northern Finland combines sustainable, natural materials with precise prefabrication techniques. The new executive suites complement Rovaniemi's beautiful yet stark scenery with white and gray furnishings, light natural wood, woven textiles, and black plumbing and lighting fixtures illuminated by ceiling-height smart windows for adjustable levels of privacy. The 3D-milled dark wood facades continue this natural aesthetic by mimicking the scales of a pinecone. Studio Puisto's tactile, arctic-inspired design continues in the hotel's new restaurant extension, which features dark, oil-stained wooden walls and a warm central fireplace. In contrast to the light-filled ArcticScene suites, this dark reception area feels like a warm hug, providing visitors immediate comfort from the often freezing weather outside. The studio's exceptional design reveals how even prefabricated construction can create grounded, mystical experiences.

The hotel's unique facade was created with 3D milling, designed to resemble the texture of a pinecone.

← ↓ Alongside a new reception area, the new extension also includes a series of executive suites.

↳ The contrasting black-and-white aesthetic of the new suites imitates the stark Arctic landscape.

Gimme Shelter

gimme shelter solutions
Väddö, Sweden

Gimme Shelter takes inspiration from Scandinavian and Japanese minimalism and functionalism for a unique take on the prefab, modular home. Emelie Holmberg's original design for the structure is composed of two discrete, enclosed sections, both of which are encircled in a continuous, covered veranda that connects them, creating an indoor-outdoor lounging and dining area in between. Modifiable versions of Gimme Shelter can encompass a range of reconfigurable modules, all surrounded by a similar patio design. Sliding wood panels move along tracks around the edges of the veranda, providing shade and privacy to outdoor portions of the home. With intervals of wooden bands, the panels contribute to the house's striking aesthetic. The vernacular style proves both elegant and functional for this distinct interpretation of prefab design.

Gimme Shelter's unpretentious style is inspired by Scandinavian and Japanese architecture.

↖← Moveable wood panels attach to tracks along the edge of the home's characteristic veranda, providing privacy and shade when needed.
↑→ Covered but unwalled veranda sections, paired with large-scale sliding glass doors for interior rooms, disrupt traditional indoor-outdoor divides.

FOCUS MATERIEN

KissKiss House

Lazor/Office
Ontario, Canada

The two main prefabricated modules that comprise KissKiss House appear to "kiss." Forming a gentle V-shape, they open onto a series of interconnected, wooden walkways elevated above the bedrock, linking house to dock house, driveway, garage, and walled vegetable garden. The complex as a whole perches at the edge of a remote Canadian lake; its materiality draws on the colors and shapes of driftwood. Each building and the exterior walkways are clad in raw white cedar, that has subsequently fully weathered driftwood grey; inside, a subtle color palette keeps to the natural hues of the landscape. Large floor-to-ceiling windows make the most of the panoramic lake view. Because the house is elevated above the lakeshore, looking out from the inside makes one feel as if they are floating above the water, the shoreline architecturally cropped from view. The distinctive floor plan also allows for moments of formal play: at the "kiss line" between modules, a polygonal sheet of glass encompasses the main entry, as if to tear open the imposing, angled walls.

KissKiss House stands on stilts near a remote Canadian lake, providing panoramic views to residents.

↓ At the “kiss line” between the house’s two primary modules stands a distinctive polygonal glass window, seemingly tearing through the wood facade.

→↘ The bay of windows overlooking the lake floods the kitchen with natural light and stunning views. Other windows offer similar views but more privacy.

East House

Peter Rose+Partners
Martha's Vineyard, MA, USA

This stately New England home cleverly uses modular design to navigate difficult terrain. Set in the Martha's Vineyard coastline—which suffers from significant coastal bluff erosion—East House's modular structure allows it to be effortlessly lifted and transported in the event of severe erosion. The residence comprises several discrete concrete boxes, each individually moveable without damage to their interior finishings. These modules connect with simple wooden corridors that can be quickly removed and rebuilt for optimally efficient transport. Beyond erosion concerns, East House attends to user comfort and aesthetics with expansive windows, soft but durable interior walls, and strategic openings that amplify ocean sounds. Sustainability is also an important concern: roofs collect rainwater for irrigation, geothermal wells regulate interior temperatures, and operable windows provide adaptable natural cooling. For East House, nature is both an opportunity and a challenge.

↖ East House is consists of eight concrete modules, each of which can be moved when the need arises.

↑ The large openings in the modules blur the boundary between architecture and greenery.

↓ East House's many windows and glass doors are carefully placed to let in ocean sounds. When opened they also allow for natural passive cooling.

→↘ Large sliding glass doors expand each room into the surrounding nature. Wood and concrete materials create a minimalist, pastoral aesthetic.

Sol to Soul

Cover
Mojave Desert,
CA, USA

Constructed with a minimalist light-gray fiber cement facade and punctuated by floor-to-ceiling windows, this prefabricated writer's refuge appears almost futuristic—a modern, pared-back outpost couched in the dramatic terrain of the Mojave Desert. The technologies used in the retreat are fittingly advanced: drones and 3D maps prevented construction from damaging the natural site; within the house, automatic shades integrate with low-emission windows to protect from the glaring desert sun; and hydronic heating and cooling minimize the home's energy footprint. In general, the house cleverly adapts to its idiosyncratic landscape, with a southern facade entirely unpenetrated by windows to shield from the main road and harsh southern sun (a design choice that makes the retreat appear even more otherworldly on approach). From the inside, however, the home feels radically open, with windows strategically positioned to frame the distinctive Mojave boulders and endless desert horizon.

The retreat's south facade is completely windowless, shielding the residence from the harsh sun.

←↙ Floor-to-ceiling windows provide unadulterated views of the Mojave Desert landscape. White minimalist interiors harmonize with these surroundings.

↓ Automatic shades pair with low-emission windows to ensure both passive and sustainable cooling, a necessity in the hot desert climate.

MRO Shack

iHouse estudio
Punta Colorada, Uruguay

Located in a quaint field not far from Uruguay's oceanic coast, MRO Shack is a calming weekend getaway prioritizing privacy while maintaining a connection to the surrounding nature. Comprised of four prefabricated modules, the cabin is a compact, simple cube that makes the most of its limited space and client constraints. Each module corresponds to a specific room or set of rooms: a bedroom, kitchen/bathroom, living room, and dining room. Each room utilizes economically selected furniture that capitalizes on the restricted square footage. Through mobile door and window panels, the cabin can alternate between closed and open modes that either protect the home's privacy or open it to the adjacent landscape. Three patios extending from each room, save the bathroom, further facilitate this natural connection. This simple, geometrical design, along with the paneled wood exterior and straightforward furniture, lend MRO Shack a snug, unpretentious air.

MRO Shack's four constitutive modules each contain one room. Patios extend from all but one of the modules.

↓ The interior is sleekly and economically designed, with the small structure containing a bedroom, living room, dining room, kitchen, and bathroom.

→↘ Simple but thoughtfully curated furnishings contribute to the cozy, unpretentious interior aesthetic, while sliding glass doors open to each of the patios.

Casa Fresnos

delavegacanolasso
Madrid, Spain

To build this cozy home, architecture firm delavegacanolasso took the ethos of a minimal construction footprint to the extreme: the house consists of three prefabricated modules designed for reduced ground impact and to preserve the surrounding forest. Casa Fresnos sits in a naturally formed void between pine trees, and its cantilevered terrace wraps around a single interrupting tree. Aesthetically, the home's wooden walls, facades, and furniture complement the neighboring environment—some parts use pine in homage to the adjacent woodland. However, the exterior's bare steel frames and whitewashed bricks prevent Casa Fresnos from fully disappearing into the landscape. Other external features—including a manufactured lily pond, a pine grove, a gravel access road, and additional flora—have a similar effect. The result is a home that respects its site both environmentally and aesthetically, trying neither to mimic nor supplant the local nature.

The house snugly fits into an existing clearing in the forest. Not a single tree was cut during construction.

↓ Large panoramic windows and a patio extend from Casa Fresnos and over the hill, looking over the dense surrounding forest.

→↘ A stepped pine and gravel pathway provides access to the house. Walls are finished with pine in homage to the adjacent woodland.

Indigo

Woonpioniers
Netherlands

Woonpioniers' prefabricated Indigo homes are all unique yet related in some ways. Each is structured around a central roof-and-wall frame that mimics the iconic gabled house shape; within certain margins, the angle of the pitched roofs can change, although the interior of the gable is always softened by a gentle, curving slope that seamlessly connects the walls and ceiling. Each prefabricated element is built with laminated timber beams and filled with cellulose insulation, constructed in a facility and later assembled on-site. This system ensures quick construction and minimal environmental impact. Within these parameters, users have immense design freedom: the standard floor plan is completely open, permitting clients to choose the number and types of rooms and levels, and the standard frame can itself be scaled to a range of sizes. As these user-specific design choices are implemented, Woonpioniers also ensures maximum sustainability, optimizing both user and environmental needs.

The iconic gabled house shape and curving interior walls typify this otherwise customizable prefab home.

← Laminated timber beams overlay the interior of each home, seamlessly connecting the ceilings and walls.

↓ In this example home, the owner customized a second level, skylights, and several lower-level rooms.

Industrialized Construction System Prototype

Ignacio Rojas Hirigoyen Architects + The Andes House
Casablanca, Chile

Inspired by the industrial age innovations of the Bauhaus, this prototype responds to rising needs for quick, low-cost, and sustainable construction. The system centers on the recycled wood fiber panel, an eco-friendly and thermally retentive material. Supported by a recycled steel structure, which is designed to be both lightweight and seismic-resistant, these panels are further linked with a system of locks and wedges composing the building's simple rectangular shape. Distinctively, a (removable) gable roof hovers over the structure, supported by thin metal trusses. This design reacts to the desert environment in which it is situated: the wide, elevated eaves permit fresh airflow, and the facade is carefully ventilated. Solar panels permit a fully off-grid electrical scheme, and the building incorporates wastewater treatment. This prefabricated, modular system is economical, sustainable, and adaptable—a veritable panacea for the construction industry's rising demands.

Recycled steel trusses and wood-fiber panels comprise the main building blocks of this modular system.

↓ The tetrahedral truss system for this prototype house supports both the building base and its gabled, removable roof.

→ Here, panels alternate with windows, providing ample natural light and passive temperature regulation.

Skyline Residence

Bohlin Cywinski Jackson
Bend, OR, USA

Located at the steep edge of a plateau dotted with Ponderosa pine trees, the Skyline Residence's long, narrow structure mimics the very horizon it so beautifully frames. Crowned with a warm wooden ceiling, buttressed by lines of beams, and furnished in colorful yet soothing hues, this charming house unpretentiously complements the stunning natural environment in which it is set. With a vast facade of windows framing the distant Cascade mountains—and an outdoor deck to maximize the view—Skyline Residence additionally highlights vistas of the dense pine forest on its opposite end, counterbalancing the sweeping scenery with the intimacy of nearby trees. Incredibly, the house was constructed in modular units with prefabricated materials, making it both expansive and economical. The residence's resulting simplicity—enhanced by the warmth of its interior design—flawlessly captures the ethos of the Pacific Northwest.

Perched at the edge of a steep plateau, the Skyline Residence captures a bird's-eye view of the forest.

↑← Windows comprise an entire wall of the home. Bare beams and trusses support the house's gently sloping roof.
→ A patio extends from the north end of the residence, providing even more direct access to the landscape.

UTZON

Retreat in the Delta

Mapa
Buenos Aires, Argentina

Mapa's Retreat in the Delta adapts to highly unusual climatic conditions: located on the banks of the Paraná Miní, a major channel of the San Fernando Delta that periodically floods, the prefabricated home must be able to withstand rushing waters and the area's humid, subtropical climate. Set on trusses that elevate the house above flood levels, Retreat in the Delta simultaneously utilizes passive bioclimatic control strategies to sustainably maximize thermal comfort. The outer walls are airtight, limiting heat transfer, and are buttressed by carefully oriented balconies that modulate the area's sunlight. The construction materials themselves similarly prioritize sustainability: the building is primarily composed of laminated wood, transported from the factory to the site on a series of small boats. In keeping with its natural setting and environmental concerns, the Retreat in the Delta is an off-grid home that applies technology to not triumph over nature, but to meld and adapt to it.

The retreat's elevated design provides access to the channel while protecting it from flooding.

↖← Covered wraparound balconies optimize views and function simultaneously as a passive cooling system. Large windows extend these views into the home.
↑→ Exposed wooden trusses elevate the retreat above flood levels. Other beams and columns are likewise left visible, creating an engineered, industrial look.

Casa Invisible

Delugan Meissl
Associated Architects
Slovenia

An expertly prefabricated, rectangular wooden structure makes up the heart of Casa Invisible, a reproducible housing unit that can be situated and modified according to each owner's needs. This core framework is designed for maximum flexibility and transportability, contributing to its uncomplicated assembly at any selected site. Its open interior layout is roughly separable into three sections, anchored by a fireplace and a "wet cell," where the bathroom and kitchen are concentrated. Besides the wet cell are an airy living room and a pleasant, secluded bedroom, which can be rearranged as desired. Barring these general structural configurations, the unit is largely customizable, from its furnishings to its facade. Prototypes installed in Slovenia make use of a stunning mirrored exterior that fuses the home with its surrounding landscape and minimalist interior design. Owners can follow these prototypes if desired, but they have free rein to adapt the home to their unique preferences.

The prototype of Casa Invisible demonstrates the home's flexibility and transportability.

↑→ Sliding glass doors and economical interior design make the house feel spacious and airy. The house's "wet cell," which holds both the bathroom and kitchen, anchors the otherwise open layout.
↠ The prototype, installed in Slovenia, features a stunning mirrored facade, lending the home its name.

ZGZ House

iHouse estudio
Blancarena, Uruguay

Two rectangular modules, joined at their longest edge, combine to form this seasonal, prefabricated cabin. Executed in an iHouse production plant and thereby shielded from climatic and terrain issues during construction, ZGZ House is an economical yet chic take on modular architecture. The cabin's dark wood exterior stands out amid the forest during the day, while its large windows, warm lighting, and tan wooden interior make it beautifully glow at night. The furniture is minimalist, sleek, and sensible, complementing the simple geometry of the building. ZGZ House's rooms are expertly arranged according to the specificities of the modular system and the constraints of the space. The bathrooms and kitchen—that is, all plumbing fixtures—are concentrated in one module. The living/dining area sits at the center of the cabin, flanked by two sets of bedrooms and bathrooms. Besides this usefully uncomplicated layout, two patios connect the home to its captivating surrounding scenery.

The house's dark wood facade and looming windows help it stand out from the surrounding landscape.

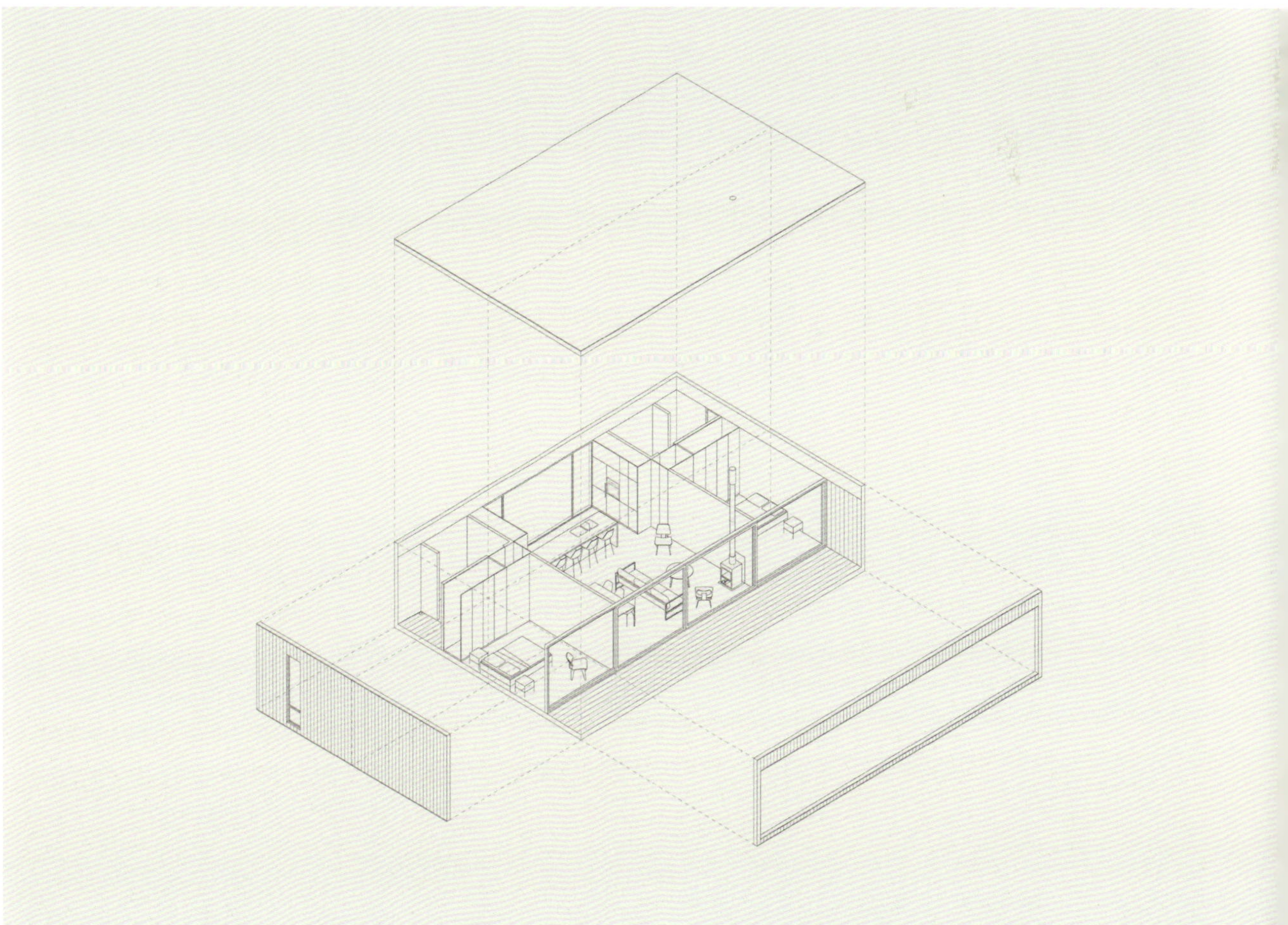

←↑ Wood interiors pair with black industrial fixtures and muted furniture to create a warm, unaffected atmosphere inside.
→ The layout is designed around a central living space, flanked on either side by bedrooms and bathrooms. All plumbing is focused in one half of the house.

Nokken Hotel Cabin

Aylott+Van Tromp
U.K.

Designed specifically for outdoor hospitality, the modular, prefabricated Nokken Hotel Cabins are built to maximize luxury and adaptability. While basic cabin templates are dressed in impeccable Nordic style, all cabins are highly customizable and can be fully designed and built within just a few months. Each original module is clad in dark stained larch wood and perforated black steel, cleverly constructed to allow underfoot plants to grow directly into the facade. The cabin walls are additionally built with eco-wool and wood pulp layering, protecting users from freezing and sweltering climates alike. Each cabin is thus thermally and aesthetically adaptable to almost any brand and site, but it is also attentive to sustainability, built with eco-friendly materials and designed with a minimal footprint. Incredibly, the Nokken Hotel Cabins provide travelers with unmediated access to nature while having little effect on the surrounding landscape.

↖ Each Nokken Hotel Cabin is clad in distinctive dark-stained larch wood and perforated black steel.

↑ A large picture window at one end of the structure permits for panoramic views wherever it is installed.

↑ Nordic interior design continues the stark simplicity of the facade into the cabin's interior, which undulates with soothing shades of black and brown.
→ The cabin's unassuming black steel facade is in fact designed for plants to grow directly into it, literally rooting the structure into its environment.

Forest Sauna

Out of the Valley
U.K.

"Scandinavians have been advocating the health benefits of saunas for years, but many people don't have room in their homes for a custom-built hot room," writes Rupert McKelvie, founder of Out of the Valley. "We hope our new saunas will inspire U.K. homeowners to embrace this Nordic tradition." The Forest Sauna is a prefabricated, purchasable sauna for gardens and outdoor spaces in the United Kingdom, rendered in sustainably sourced wood. The external black larch wood is charred using an ancient Japanese technique called *shou sugi ban,* and the interior is clad in thermo-alder wood. The lumber is fitted around a raised steel chassis using a combination of traditional and modern construction methods that are executed in a Devon workshop and then transported to the chosen site. Inside, two wooden benches seating four flank a central heater. An enormous window integrates the tranquility of the surrounding environment, and a cold shower can be added to the sauna's solemn, unpretentious exterior.

The sauna's textured facade is created using an ancient Japanese charring technique called *shou sugi ban*.

←↙ Each sauna contains two benches and a heater and can seat up to four people. A cold shower can also be attached to the structure's external wall.

↓ A large window dominates one wall of the sauna, ensuring that users can luxuriate in the surrounding scenery while relaxing in the heat.

Portable Cabin

wiercinski-studio
Poznan, Poland

Constructed out of two adapted shipping containers, the Portable Cabin is a delightful experiment in temporary, mobile architecture responding to the recent rise of remote work. Currently located in a community garden in Poznan, the cabin includes a living room, kitchen, workspace, bedroom, and bathtub as well as a furnished terrace. The interior walls are insulated with spray foam and finished with birch plywood while the facade consists of sheet metal painted in a muted green color to mimic the surrounding greenery. Floor-to-ceiling glass doors open to the terrace, flooding the warm, homey interior with natural light. Considerations, such as facade color and furniture placement, respond directly to the current site, but these design choices can be modified depending on location. In the future, the Portable Cabin will travel to a forest and finally to water, testing its mobility and adaptability to different terrains.

The muted moss green of cabin's facade was selected specifically to harmonize with the site.

BIURO
OFFICE

←↙ Sliding glass doors connect the cabin interior to a terrace with furniture and potted plants. Walls are finished with birch plywood, creating a soft, warm atmosphere.

↓ Portable Cabin was partially placed on the roof of previously standing containers, which serve as storage space for the community garden in Poznan, Poland.

Minimod Curucaca

Mapa
Curucaca, Brazil

Mapa combined some of the newest technologies—cross-laminated wood, digitally milled wood paneling, and advanced prefabrication—to create a homey, light-filled abode in a forest clearing in southern Brazil. Combining natural materials, floor-to-ceiling glass doors, and even a green roof, Minimod both blends into the natural environment and lets the magnificent views seep through its rooms. The house utilizes a relatively open layout with variable privacy afforded to the bedrooms and bathrooms, allowing the light and scenery from the glass doors and windows to stretch across the entire length of the home. Two patios facilitate the house's connection to the surrounding forest as well. Minimod was prefabricated off-site, brought to the clearing via a truck, and completed on-site. As a result of this process, the house's construction was highly efficient, sustainable, and suitable to the remote, rugged environment. It is simultaneously technically advanced and a sublime natural retreat.

Floor-to-ceiling sliding glass doors allow natural views to sweep through the relatively open-plan home.

HIDE AND SEEK

↖← Uniform wood ceilings, floors, and walls ensconce the spare furnishings and fixtures, mixing natural and industrial aesthetics to great effect.
↑→ Besides the large windows and patio connecting users to the surrounding landscape, Minimod also includes a green roof, further integrating house and forest.

Mazzini House

iHouse estudio
Punta Ballena,
Uruguay

Mazzini House brings a contemporary, "prefab" twist to classic midcentury modern design. Constructed in a forest in Punta Ballena, this open-plan rectangular home immerses its users in the surrounding nature, sporting floor-to-ceiling windows, glass sliding doors, and a furnished outdoor patio. There are almost no doors separating the rooms inside, with only two yellow "blocks"—which contain the kitchen, bathrooms, and storage—roughly demarcating the two bedrooms and living room. As a result, circulation through the space follows the rhythms of the forest, uninhibited besides the free-standing blocks and smatterings of furniture. Even with its impressively formulated design, Mazzini House was entirely prefabricated, built, and assembled in an iHouse production plant. This approach, central to the studio's practice, allowed for quick construction and higher-quality assembly even though the house design is completely unique.

The elongated shape and minimalist interior design of Mazzini House derive from midcentury modernism.

←↙ Yellow "blocks" contain the kitchen, bathroom, and storage. A circular bedroom window epitomizes the elegant whimsy of the house's design.

↓ Large sliding glass doors extend across two walls, offering views of the forest accompanied by curtains for privacy.

House Mael

iHouse estudio
Sierra de Minas, Uruguay

House Mael is modular and prefabricated, but it caters to its extraordinary site with stunning success. The house is set in a rural landscape dominated by wide plains, low mountains, densely scattered rocks, and soaring skies. The low, wide, rectangular building mimics its squat surrounding mountains, with a dark wood exterior to match the rocky slopes. Floor-to-ceiling sliding glass doors and wide, covered patios frame the view, which is deliberately visible from almost every room. Architects Andrés Garcia and Marcelo Mederos describe the building as "designed from the outside in." A central kitchen, dining, and living room stretches the entire length of the house, connecting the two patios and providing an unobstructed sightline through the building. The white paneled walls, warm wooden ceiling, and neutrally colored furniture harmonize with the view. While the bedrooms are comparatively private, each boasts a full wall of glass providing access to the spectacular scenery.

The low, flat design of House Mael echoes the squat mountains and wide plains of its surrounding environment.

↞↙ Spacious common areas connect both ends of the home, providing a continuous sightline through most of the interior. Warm tones evoke an inviting aura.
←↓ The covered patios on either end provide shading and frame stunning natural views. They also extend the wood plank finishing of the interior.

Vipp Shelter

Vipp
Lake Immeln, Sweden

Vipp, a Danish company that originally specialized in steel object design, developed their Vipp Shelter in 2014 as a luxurious natural getaway. Because of the firm's experience in industrial design, the prefabricated getaway is meticulously constructed and finished to an acute level of detail. Vipp entirely predetermined and arranged the beautiful black steel frame and furnishings, which are punctuated by floor-to-ceiling glass windows and skylights. Buyers only have to select a placement location and their involvement in the construction, and the design process is complete. In 2017, a Vipp Shelter was constructed at Lake Immeln for short-term vacation stays. Its austere design keeps the focus on the surrounding nature, and its largest window perfectly frames the nearby lake. The shelter's open plan and numerous skylights immerse guests in the landscape at all times. Maybe, it seems to suggest, industrial steel and nature aren't such opposites after all.

↖ Cabins are adaptable to a variety of sites. This shelter was constructed at Lake Immeln in Sweden.

↑ Vipp Shelter's black steel frame exemplifies the company's long-standing expertise in steel object design.

↓ Large skylights and floor-to-ceiling windows open Vipp Shelter to the surrounding natural views.

→↘ The cabin comes entirely predesigned, with furnishings meticulously fabricated to match the space.

vipp

Topol 27

DublDom
Zhukovsky District,
Russia

This cabin's minimal yet classical gabled house shape could complement almost any site. Designed to be fully prefabricated—buyers can grab their Topol 27 from a warehouse and finish installing it within a day—these structures are primed to not just be usable, but portable and adaptable to diverse locations, too. This installation on a riverbank in Russia orients its full-wall bedside window toward the river and forest, optimizing the view and the bedroom's privacy. All Topol 27s cover 290 square feet (27 square meters) of space—hence the project's name. There are five main areas within each home: a bedroom, a kitchen, a living room, a bathroom, and a dressing room. Each room is fully functional by the time it leaves the warehouse, with appliances, furniture, dishes, cutlery, and lighting pre-installed. Furnishings are carefully selected to be eco-friendly, wear-resistant, and, of course, tasteful. Natural oak and black metal pair with stone countertops and glass, which beautifully reflects the outside scenery.

Topol 27's sleek take on the iconic gabled house shape is constructed in natural oak wood and black metal.

↓ All furniture, appliances, dishes, and cutlery are pre-installed so that the cabin is instantly operable. The interior combines wood with metal accents.

→↘ One end of Topol 27 is capped with a beautiful picture window. Here, it is oriented toward the nearby river and woodland, providing the bedroom with further privacy.

Cabin Anna

Caspar Schols
De Biesbosch
National Park,
Netherlands

Caspar Schols designed the first iteration of this structure as a private garden cabin for his mother, constructed with sliding walls to allow for maximum flexibility and a fluid connection with nature. When his design gained widespread renown, he developed Cabin Anna, a prefabricated and streamlined version of his initial garden cabin that can be built (and rebuilt) anywhere. Cabin Anna is designed not just to adapt to a variety of environments, but to change breezes, sunlight, and other facets of nature with its sliding wood walls. Private interiors can transform into open platforms with a single push, allowing users to fully immerse themselves in the surrounding environment. Importantly, due to its prefabricated and sustainable design, the construction and functioning of the home minimally impact nature—even that of the immediate site. Multiple cabins currently comprise a resort in Holenberg, Netherlands, but individual cabins can also be purchased for long-term living.

Cabin Anna's sliding walls allow users to decide how immersed they want to be in nature at any moment.

←↓ The cabin includes three "shells." Two of which slide along tracks: one glass and two wood and steel. The "shells" can overlap or open completely, permitting a variety of configurations with varying privacy. → The design stands out for its exposed wooden trusses, which provide strong structural integrity and lend the cabin its artisanal, crafted look.

← The design contains all amenities needed for functional living, including a kitchen, bedroom, and bathroom.
↑ Kitchen and bathroom furnishings are made of stainless steel. Cabins built in the Netherlands can also be modified to be fully off-grid and self-sufficient.

←↓ The mobile sections slide on industrial wheels along built-in tracks and can be rearranged simply by pulling them into the desired location. → Cabin Anna is primarily made of sustainable Accoya wood. Because it is relatively light, it can be installed in most places using only a screw foundation.

Bjellandsbu-Åkrafjorden Cabin

Snøhetta
Etne, Norway

One family has maintained a farm in the foothills of the Åkrafjorden for generations, transporting sheep between the water's edge of this Norwegian fjord and an adjacent mountain plateau every year, adapting to the changing seasons. The Bjellandsbu-Åkrafjorden Cabin provides shelter atop the plateau, offering rest and warmth to the shepherds after their grueling walks through potentially volatile weather conditions. The distinctive cabin sinks into the low, rolling hills of the highland, camouflaged by stone and grass; for much of the year, it is shrouded under a deep layer of snow. A layer of hand-cut pine logs constitutes the cabin's unusual, sloping shape supported by two steel beams. From the inside, the shelter is just one large room: functions of a bedroom, living room, and kitchen combine into one spacious volume, with the furniture gathered around a central hearth. Designed to facilitate family gatherings, the cabin can in fact sleep 21 people at once, a fact belied by its humble, unassuming exterior.

The cabin's curving, sloped shape and use of natural materials nod to the surrounding rolling hills.

← The cabin is built from hand-cut pine logs and glass; it is crowned with grass and buttressed with raw stone.
↑ The shelter contains just one large room organized around a central hearth.
→ Designed to meld seamlessly into the landscape, from afar the cabin may resemble just another upturned rock.

Igluhut

Iglucraft
Estonia

The huts and saunas that Iglucraft offers combine a centuries-old shingling technique with a unique, cylindrical hut shape, in effect sheathing their prefabricated construction with an artisanal facade. This unlikely but stunning combination hearkens to the company's founding ideas, which emphasize the importance of slowing down, thinking, and spending time with oneself. With their craft-like quality, the insular structures bring these ideals to the fore: one could imagine unwinding in one of the huts, soothed by its curved ceiling and walls. In fact, the designers used this motif of round forms to counter the rigidity imposed by most linear cityscapes—although, for the Iglusaunas, the domed roof serves the additional function of trapping and moving steam downward. To complement the handmade quality of each hut and sauna, buyers also have the option of customization. Each Iglucraft structure comes with options for paint color, size, and window type.

The vernacular shingling technique that sheathes each Igluhut conceals its prefabricated construction.

←↙ The Igluhut's cylindrical shape, round ceilings, and arched windows utilize soothing, curving forms as a respite from the rigid linearity of city architecture.

↓ The muted color palette, pastoral design, and craft-like quality of the residential huts encourage users to wind down and relax inside.

↓ The domed shape of the Iglusauna helps trap rising steam and recirculate it downward, keeping the humidity and temperature inside uniform.

→↘ Owners can customize the size of their Igluhuts and Iglusaunas. Shown here are the Single and Triple Iglusauna models, seating four and six people.

Bert

Studio Precht & Baumbau
Austria

Studio Precht's modular treehouse, Bert, designed for the tiny-homes startup Baumbau, loosely imitates the forms of a forest. The shingles resemble leaves but remain natural shades of brown, while the dark, cozy center and open, light-filled "branches" mimic the varied atmospheres of the forest floor itself. With these quirky, branching modules, Studio Precht discards conventional building types and approaches design with the openness of a child. Lounging in one of the circular branches, guests can imagine themselves as birds perched in the lush canopy. Bert's modular, prefabricated design allows buyers to customize the scale of each treehouse as desired. The structure's vertical stacking and room-sized branches leave a minimal footprint on the nature being enjoyed, and each iteration is totally self-sufficient with solar panels, a composting toilet, and a water treatment facility. With Bert's nature-inspired design, of course nature itself is protected.

↖ The treehouse is organized around a central column from which cylindrical rooms protrude like branches.

↑ Users lounging in one of the "branches" may imagine themselves as birds perched in a tree canopy.

←↙ The relative darkness and privacy of the core stairwell is complemented by the open, light-filled rooms that extend from the central column.

↓ "Branches" are typically capped either with floor-to-ceiling windows or furnished patios, allowing residents to look out onto the forest canopy.

←↓ The dark interiors, punctuated by light from the windows, mimic the feeling of walking along the forest floor as sunlight streams through leaves.
→ Bert's modular construction permits the treehouse to extend to varying heights while leaving the same minimal footprint of just the central column.

Space of Mind

Studio Puisto
Finland

Designed and prototyped during the height of Covid-19, Space of Mind—as its name implies—provides a space to escape the hustle and bustle of home and work life, prompted by the claustrophobia many felt during the pandemic. Recognizing that people find comfort in widely different ways, the mini cabin's modular design ensures maximum adaptability: it can be a spare bedroom, a gym, a home office, and more. The interior is designed with versatility in mind, too, with custom furniture that attaches to prefabricated rungs. Moreover, the small size and light weight ensure that Space of Mind can be placed anywhere, as it can be transported by a helicopter or crane if necessary. The design, while simple and constructed with raw Finnish wood, remains stylish and soothing with its irregular form and a large window. Almost gem-like in shape, Space of Mind beautifully embellishes gardens, roofs, or any other site it's placed in.

← Space of Mind's small size, light weight, and prefab construction make it suitable for almost any site.

↑ The cabin's wall-sized window ensures that residents have ample natural light and, potentially, a view.

↓ Designed in an irregular, gem-like shape, the structure's unique form belies its economical construction.

→ Modular, custom, rearrangeable furniture attaches to prefabricated rungs inside the mini cabin.

OM1

Dimensions X
Australia

Peter Stutchbury's ambitious Dimensions X project addresses the increasing need for sustainable housing. Its first model, OM1, is a flexible, prefabricated housing unit composed of combinable, customizable modules. Sub-designs ranging from OM1-1 to OM1-4 merge one to four of these compact modules respectively, with each bay divisible into two rooms with specifiable functions. All predesigned rooms optimize storage and space through tasteful, rustic-chic design. This level of optimization reduces the resources spent—each build is quick and carbon negative—and makes OM1 highly adaptable. All units are personally configurable, relocatable, and modifiable according to the precise needs of different users and sites. Each OM1 house shares key facets: integrated solar and battery-powered energy; a water collection system; low-energy fittings; and high energy-efficiency. OM1 units may also incorporate open patios and large windows, integrating its users with their natural surroundings.

↖ OM1's predesigned room options, though modifiable, feature a distinct rustic-chic aesthetic.

↑ Owners can choose the cabin's size, customize its contents, and select add-ons such as skylights.

BRIGITTE

↖← Units may contain one to four modules, each of which can hold up to two rooms. The future residents configure room placement according to their preferences.
↑→ When customizing their cabin, users can select the size of doors and windows and choose where to place them. They may also choose to add a deck.

Retreat in Finca Aguy

Mapa
Pueblo Edén, Uruguay

Situated at the edge of an isolated olive field, the Retreat in Finca Aguy responds to the environmental and practical challenges of remote rural living. Prefabricated in a factory and later transported 125 miles (200 km) to Pueblo Edén, the house limits its impact on its beautiful natural setting, minimizing ground disturbance and drastically reducing material waste through high-precision construction. A design that harmonizes with the magnificent scenery complements the sustainable approach: the building's natural wooden interiors, black furniture accents, gray corrugated exterior, and rusticated stone retaining walls coordinate with the surrounding environment while still allowing the house to stand out. Likewise, sliding wood panels open to a patio and offer unobstructed views of the hills, sky, and shrubbery. While utilizing highly efficient prefabrication techniques, the Retreat in Finca Aguy retains exquisite aesthetics and flexibly adapts to the needs of its users.

The retreat's rural site raised construction and design challenges that the architects solved with prefabrication.

←↙ The house's warm wooden ceilings and walls, matched with sleek black accents, cultivate an inviting yet modern interior aesthetic.

↓ The retreat's corrugated metal facade counterpoises the rusticated stone wall upon which it sits, beautifully juxtaposing industrial and natural styles.

Introduction

A

B

C

D

G

I

ZGZ House
Blancarena, Uruguay
Senior Architects:
Luciana Cano, Agustin Sica
Partners: Andres Garcia,
Marcelo Mederos
Photography: Aldo Lanzi /
aldolanzi.com / @aldo.lanzi
pp. 170–175

Mazzini House
Punta Ballena, Uruguay
Senior Architects:
Luciana Cano, Agustin Sica
Partners: Andres Garcia,
Marcelo Mederos
Photography: Aldo Lanzi /
aldolanzi.com / @aldo.lanzi
pp. 192–197

House Mael
Sierra de Minas, Uruguay
Senior Architects:
Luciana Cano, Agustin Sica
Partners: Andres Garcia,
Marcelo Mederos
Photography: Aldo Lanzi /
aldolanzi.com / @aldo.lanzi
pp. 198–203

J

Jean-Benjamin Maneval CHZON
chzon.com

Bubble House
Vexin, France
Photography: Karel Balas / Vega Mg
pp. 038–041

K

KOSMOS
k-s-m-s.com

"Tin Can" Castle
Georgia
Photography: Polina Lomilina
pp. 050–051

L

Larrou Arq
larrou.com / @larrou_arq

AKA Patagonia
Puerto Natales, Chile
Photography: alesondelvillar /
alesondelvillar.com /
@alesondelvillar.photoarch
pp. 096–099

Lazor / Office
lazoroffice.com

KissKiss House
Ontario, Canada
Design Team: Charlie Lazor,
Morgan Peterson
Photography: Peter Von De Linde /
vondelinde.com
pp. 120–123

M

MAPA
mapaarq.com

Retreat in the Delta
Buenos Aires, Argentina
Partners: Luciano Andrades,
Matías Carballal, Andrés Gobba,
Mauricio López, Silvio Machado
Executive Development and
Construction Management:
Joaquín Berdes
Interior Design: Solsken
Photography: Leonardo Finotti /
leonardofinotti.com
pp. 160–165

Minimod Curucaca
Curucaca, Brazil
Partners: Luciano Andrades,
Matías Carballal, Andrés Gobba,
Mauricio López, Silvio Machado
Assembly and Production: Crosslam
Photography: Leonardo Finotti /
leonardofinotti.com
pp. 188–191

Retreat in Finca Aguy
Pueblo Edén, Uruguay
Partners: Luciano Andrades, Matías
Carballal, Rochelle Castro, Andrés
Gobba, Mauricio López, Silvio Machado
Construction and Installation: Nebimol
Interior Design: BoConcept
Photography: Leonardo Finotti /
leonardofinotti.com
pp. 248–253

MAST
mast.dk

Land on Water
Lake Constance, Austria
Project design: MAST,
Hubert Rhomberg & Fragile
Renders: KVANT-1 / kvant1.no
pp. 092–094,
Mast
p. 095

O

Ofis Architects
ofis.si

Living Unit
Ljubljana, Slovenia
Photography: Tomaž Gregorič
and Janez Martinčič
pp. 016–021

Out of the Valley
outofthevalley.co.uk

Forest Sauna
U.K.
Photography: OLCO Studio /
olcostudios.com / @olcostudios
pp. 180–183

P

Peter Rose + Partners
roseandpartners.com

East House
Martha's Vineyard, MA, USA
Photography: Chuck Choi
pp. 124–131

Pin-Up Houses
pinuphouses.com

Gaia
Czech Republic
Architect: Vojtech Valda
Photography: Jakub Zdechovan /
zdechovan.studio / @zdechovan.studio
pp. 022–027

S

ŠA Atelier
sarkauskai.com

019 Cabin
Apple Island, Lithuania
Lead Architects:
Gabrielė Šarkauskienė
and Antanas Šarkauskas
Client: MB "Piritas"
Structural Engineer: Evaldas Šemeta
Photography: Vaidotas Darulis
pp. 012–013, 014 top, 015,
Gabriele Sarkauskiene
p. 014 bottom

Schemata Workshop
schemataworkshop.com

Kirkland Avenue Homes
Renton, WA, USA
Civil Engineer and Landscape
Architects: SvR Design Company
(now MIG)
Structural Engineer: DCI Engineers
Modular Manufacturer:
Champion Commercial Structures
Photography:
William Wright Photography
pp. 060–063

Snøhetta
snohetta.com

Bjellandsbu-Åkrafjorden Cabin
Etne, Norway
Photography: James Silverman /
jamessilverman.co.uk /
@jamessilvermanphoto
pp. 222–225

Studio Precht & Baumbau
precht.at / baumbau.at

Bert
Austria
Renders: Courtesy of Studio Precht
pp. 232, 234 bottom right, 235, 236 top
Photography: Christian Flatscher /
christianflatscher.com
pp. 233, 234 top & bottom left,
236 bottom, 237

Studio Puisto
studiopuisto.fi

Uni Kanava Resort
Oravi, Finland
Photography: Marc Goodwin /
Archmospheres / archmospheres.com
pp. 104–107

Arctic TreeHouse Hotel
Rovaniemi, Finland
Photography: Riikka Kantinkoski /
riikkakantinkoski.com
pp. 108–113

Space of Mind
Finland
Photography: Marc Goodwin /
Archmospheres / archmospheres.com
pp. 238–240, 242–243
Render: Studio Puisto
p. 241

SUMMARY
summary.pt

1000 m² Prefabricated Housing
Vale de Cambra, Portugal
Project Leader: Samuel Gonçalves
Project Team: Inês Vieira Rodrigues
(project manager), Gonçalo
Vaz de Carvalho, Maria João Freitas
Photography: FG+SG Fernando
Guerra + Sérgio Guerra /
ultimasreportagens.com
pp. 088–091

V

Vipp
vipp.com

Vipp Shelter
Lake Immeln, Sweden
Photography: Rasmus Hjortshøj /
rasmushjortshoj.com
pp. 204–209

W

wiercinski-studio

Portable Cabin
Poznan, Poland
Photography: ONI Studio / oni.com.pl
pp. 184–187

William Samuels Architects
williamsamuels.co.nz

Studio House
Nelson, New Zealand
Photography: Simon Devitt /
simondevitt.com
pp. 046–049

Woonpioniers
woonpioniers.nl

Sprout
Netherlands
Photography: Jonah Samyn /
jonahsamyn.be
pp. 052–055

Indigo
Netherlands
Photography: Henny van Belkom /
vanbelkomproducties.nl
pp. 146–149

Z

ZIKZAK Architects
zikzakarchitects.com

Revival
Ukraine
Renders: ZIKZAK Architects
pp. 064–067

Prefab and Modular

Prefabricated Houses and Modular Architecture

This book was conceived, edited, and designed by gestalten.

Edited by Robert Klanten and Masha Erman

Editorial support by Effie Efthymiadi

Introduction by José Tomás Franco (pp. 4–11)
Project texts and captions by Yves Cao

Editorial Management: Arndt Jasper
Photo Editor: Madeline Dudley-Yates

Design, layout, and cover by Melanie Ullrich

Typeface: IBM Plex Serif and IBM Plex Mono by Mike Abbink and Bold Monday

Cover image: Bert by Studio Precht & Baumbau, photo by Christian Flatscher
Backcover image: Vipp Shelter by Vipp, photo by Rasmus Hjortshøj

Printed by Grafisches Centrum Cuno, Calbe, Germany
Made in Europe

Published by gestalten, Berlin 2024
ISBN 978-3-96704-124-8

For more information, and to order books, please visit www.gestalten.com

Bibliographic information published by the Deutsche Nationalbibliothek.
The Deutsche Nationalbibliothek lists this publication in the Deutsche Nationalbibliografie; detailed bibliographic data is available online at www.dnb.de

None of the content in this book was published in exchange for payment by commercial parties or designers; the inclusion of all work is based solely on its artistic merit.

This book was printed on paper certified according to the standards of the FSC®.

FSC www.fsc.org
MIX
Paper from responsible sources
FSC® C043106